STRESS REDUCTION

9 Recipes To Inspire You To Make Your Life Better After Divorce

Table of Contents

INTRODUCTION

Across several millenniums, marriage has evolved to become one of the most significant and most lasting institutions in the history of humankind. The voluntary union of two separate individuals to live together as equal partners who share emotions, love, care, affection, dreams, and hopes while possibly producing and raising offspring has been the only true common denominator among the different cultures, ages and race to have graced this planet.

Ideally, marriage is meant as a lasting relationship between the two partners that meant to be broken only in the event of the death of one of the partners, but unfortunately, it doesn't always work out that way. Nobody sets on a marriage with the intention of breaking up ties later, but for a plethora of different reasons, spouses might find it prudent to break up their marriage and become single once again. Enters divorce!!! What do the divorce rates say?

Approximately 50% of marriages eventually end up in a divorce.

20% of first marriages end in a divorce in the first five years.

60% of second marriages end in divorce.

73% of third marriages end in divorce.

Every 13 seconds, there is one divorce in America.

The time it will take you to see Titanic, there would have been about 850 divorces.

The rates show how divorce has become a common occurrence. They show that despite our best intentions, many marriages are been destined for the rocks. The breakup of marriages can have a quite devastating effect, especially on women. The end of a marriage does not only mean the end of a partnership you had hoped to enjoy for a long time, but it also signifies the end of a long list of hopes, aspirations, dreams, and visions for the future. It means you can no longer count on support from the individual you probably relied most upon. To most people, it also means they need to delete some of the fondest memories and recollections they have ever had. These, the pressure of having to learn a new lifestyle and adjusting to the realities can prove to be quite a heavy burden that not everybody can easily carry. A lot of people crumble under the weight of the new expectations and lifestyle; many people never learn to truly overcome their marriage and yet, many others still hold on to the vestiges of their former partner.

In spite of all these, though, a fraction of divorced women has learned to quickly rise and grow beyond the supposed limits divorce places in their paths. They have refused to be weighed down by the pressures inherent after a divorce. They have not merely managed to survive, they have decided to thrive and move on. How did they manage it? By dealing with **STRESS**!!!

Stress, physical and mental, is the greatest negative effect a divorce can introduce in your life. Stress isn't exactly bad. In fact, it is a protective system put in place by the body to protect us from getting overwhelmed by physical, mental and physiological factors including our thoughts, worry, anxiety, depression, and overall attitude. However, when stress exceeds a certain level or becomes a persistent feature of your life, it turns bad very quickly. It can quickly overload the brain and clog up your entire life. It can destroy confidence, turn you into a social recluse, lower your irritability threshold, and totally affect your relationships. Unfortunately, being the 'deeper' sex, women are more prone to the negative effects of stress after a divorce.

This is why I have written this book; to enable you to learn the secrets of defeating the emotional and mental stress that divorces introduce in the lives of women. There some proven ways you can learn to shoo away stress after divorce, heal the mental wounds of a recent separation and repair your psyche in a bid to leave yourself open and receptive to develop new, healthy connections and relationships. I will deal extensively with the nine most important reasons and ways for you to get over the failed promises, mistakes, and dashed hopes that come with a broken marriage. Take your time to read through and implement the tips. They will help you defeat or at least, cope better with the extra stress associated with the post-marriage period.

CHAPTER 1

LET IT GO AND TURN THE PAGE.

So, you have just gotten divorced, and you can't seem to let go of the thoughts and memories of your partner? You keep remembering the good times, and find yourself reminiscing all the time about how and where it all went wrong? Do you maybe even have a lingering hope that he may suddenly have a change of heart or attitude, and you may have the wonderful life you dreamt of before getting married? If these thoughts mirror your current pattern of thinking, well, let me jolt you out of it. **"He is NOT COMING BACK"!!!**

Repeat that to yourself each time you find your thoughts wandering along these paths. In fact, take a pen and write it out as many times as possible each time your mind drifts off. That is the first step in developing a new lease of life; accepting that the marriage is truly and well over. You do nobody any good by keeping your wounds fresh; not you, not your kids and definitely not HIM!!!

Understand that you were not the fault:

Many women become so attached to their partners that they simply make up excuses for them. In fact, even after a divorce, they subconsciously still heap a majority of the responsibility on their shoulders. This means, they cannot move onto the next chapter in their life. Often, however, before a divorce can materialize, both partners must have contributed to the breakdown. One of the best ways to reach closure is by understanding that some people are unmanageable, and situations can escalate and get out of hands. Give yourself breathing space. Do not fall into the trap of self-blame.

Do not keep souvenirs:

Most times, the reason we buy or keep souvenirs is to remember specific incidents or days. Keeping souvenirs that directly remind you of the happiest moments of your marriage, and your husband can keep your heart bleeding long after the marriage is over. It is best to keep such in places where you don't run into them all the time to give yourself some needed space.

Keep a healthy distance away:

I am not asking you to run away or vacate your house, but do not take up residence on the same street as your immediate past husband. It spells danger and pain. Keeping him in view is a fresh jab to your wound and memories. Do not stalk him or plan to run into him. By all means, do not change your life entirely to avoid him; no man is worth that. But, keep him away from sight (and consequently mind) by limiting the number of times you come in contact all the time, at least, when the divorce process is still relatively fresh in your mind.

CHAPTER 2

CELEBRATE YOUR FREEDOM AND LEARN HOW TO USE IT

Most times, most women seem to only see the words "separation" and "loneliness" when they think of their divorce. In fact, these two words help some women delay the inevitable and cause them more pain than is necessary. Instead of these words, you can choose instead to see the other side of the coin; "freedom". Yes, divorce may mean that you are now separated, and you may get a bit lonely especially in the immediate period after it. But by all means, do not fail to realize that this means you are **FREE**. Now, depending on you, 'free' can either mean more time for desolation, reminiscing about missed opportunities and dreams. Or 'free' can mean you have more time to yourself; to improve and become a better version of yourself. You can choose to realize that you have fewer commitments and do not necessarily have to make the same sacrifices you have been making to accommodate your partner's wish and goals. The choice is yours.

Choosing to recognize that you are free now more than ever, however, also comes with the added responsibility of using your new freedom to improve your personality. How can you do this?

Work on yourself esteem:

Your new found freedom is not a ticket to lay low. It is not a free pass to the "low self-esteem" bus. Do not allow your divorce to cower you into looking to please every other person in sight or depend on their approval to feel good about yourself. That will only bring you more stress. Instead, allow it to spur you to hold your head high, and be confident in your abilities.

Do not make the same mistake:

If you have detected certain faults in your character, now is the best time to deal with them without external influence. Work on your weaknesses to improve even better. If you had gotten married for the wrong reasons, do not make the same mistake of choosing the wrong priorities after divorce. Instead, focus on not repeating the same mistakes.

Do not keep the door open:

Do not commit what I call the 'grievous' mistake. Do not leave the door ajar hoping for a return from your former husband. Instead, close that door firmly and politely. Your kids (if any) may mean that you get to constantly meet each other, but instead of hanging onto his coattails for the second round of disappointment, open the windows and let a fresh lease come into your life.

Avoid picking up bad habits:

freedom with a bit of confusion is the perfect recipe to weaken most people's resolve and discipline; the combination can invite you to pick up new, destructive habits like procrastination, alcoholism, and gambling. Avoiding them is a must if you must keep your life on a steady path.

CHAPTER 3

SELF-LOVE; TAKING CARE OF

YOURSELF

I f you do not take care of yourself, who will? You owe yourself a right of taking care of yourself. No matter how strong your bonds are, nobody else can take good care of your life as you can. It can be hard if you have depended on your spouse for certain aspects of your life. But there must have been a reason why you could proceed no further with your marriage. If that reason was good enough to cut off your marriage, then, it is good enough to assume responsibility for your life.

Taking good care of you after a divorce is a complex task. You may not be entirely sure of what you even want, and this may bring on a lot of worry, anxiety, and depression into your life. These may even threaten your sleep and health, and you may be tempted to let things slide out of your hand, but do not create even more problems. Instead, pay even greater attention to understanding yourself and ensuring you are in better shape than ever. You absolutely need it, to help you take good care of yourself;

Expect and adjust to new realities:

Life after divorce is an entirely new world devoid of some of the securities and landmarks you had planted earlier in life. Expect to see things in a new light; the trick is in learning to adjust to whatever new situation that may arise. Avoid getting overwhelmed by the new factors creeping into your life.

Don't fight your feelings:

You have the right to be confused or a bit overwhelmed after a divorce. Do not fight these feelings or feel depressed about them. Instead, understand them and work on eliminating them. It is no crime to be down for a little bit; the only sin is remaining down and out.

Live a healthy lifestyle:

More than you have ever done, you need to focus on remaining healthy than before. The stress brought upon by a divorce can task your physical limits, but you need to adopt habits that can help you stay ahead constantly. Avoiding dangerous addictions such as substance abuse, alcoholism and smoking, take on an added importance. Your kids may need more attention now more than ever, and you simply cannot undermine or decrease the quality of your health if you are to be there to provide it for them.

CHAPTER 4
SELF-IMPROVEMENT THROUGH ACTIVITIES

One of the best ways to take your mind off worries and anxiety is engaging in more and meaningful activities that can keep you occupied, and give you a new focus. Yes, you have more free time, and devoting some of it to engaging activities you enjoy can help stave off the psychological pressure of being alone. It is the right time for you to get involved in sports and other activities that stimulate the brain vigorously.

Aside from the enjoyment and thrills of being engaged in sports and such activities, they will bring you in contact with more people, and provide you with a fresh purpose in life. There is no such a healing balm for divorce situations than a fresh purpose and activities to look forward to. Other activities you can consider include:

Exercising more:

Exercise gives you better health and makes you feel more confident about your physique and yourself. Taking out a little time to sweat it out in the gym or run around the park can help a lot to help boost your immunity towards stress, and various other psychological distresses.

Keeping a diary and reading books:

I know not everybody is quite comfy with the idea of keeping a diary; some can't even summon the energy to do so, but it could be a great pastime to help you derive comfort. It is like pouring out your heart to somebody else. Being able to look at your life from an outsider's perspective while read your diary can help you gain new perspectives and draw strength. Books can be a great help. Self-help and motivational books like this one can help you with new tips and ideas for your life, and reading them can be of great help. Even fiction books can help give you a clean mind, and provide extra enjoyment if you fancy them.

Joining a Support Group:

Meeting people with the same problems as us has always been a great relief for humans. Nowadays, there are support groups for almost all kinds of situations and problems, and recovery from a divorce is not left out. Socializing with people with the same issues can help awaken you to the fact that you are not alone in the world. In fact, it can make you forget your worries in the presence of people with bigger ones.

CHAPTER 5

SELF-DEVELOPMENT; GIVING YOUR MIND NEW CONTENT

ivorce is a time of doubt. Accusations, fault, and blame are been laid at each partner's feet and no matter how strong you may be psychologically, there is no escaping some modicum of the doubt especially if some of these are true. However, you can't continue to still live with these doubts about your own abilities and character after your divorce, if you intend to move on completely. It is easier to ignore them, but the best way to fix them is by immersing yourself in productive endeavors that can prove to you that you have greater value than you are given credit for. By taking on new skills, courses and smoothen the cracks in your personality, you can build up a better version of yourself, and better equipped to deal with whatever life throws at you. You can self-develop by;

Setting new goals and aims:

There is no greater motivation than a new challenge or goal. It doesn't matter if it is work related or personal; get yourself new targets to work towards. Decide to finally try your hands at that new business idea you have always hard. Sitting around idle gives stress, and negative thoughts the right channel they need to creep into your life. Instead, channel your energy towards a more productive end like a new personal milestone in efficiency, and set up a chart to measure your improvement.

Learning new skills and knowledge:

Marriage can leave us totally absorbed and with little time left to engage our creative talents. Divorce leaves us with some more free time. What does that tell us? Divorce gives us more time to invest our cognitive and mental ability into acquiring more skills and knowledge to become even better at work. It isn't even necessarily worked; it could be something like nurturing your artistic talents or trying out your hands at blogging or painting. Whatever you do is okay.

CHAPTER 6

SELF-MOTIVATION; LOOK INSIDE

YOU

How can you learn to protect yourself from some of the harshest criticism and self-doubt that may come your way during and after a divorce? Simply by looking inwards! To prevent other people from being able to injure your sensibilities, you need to be in tune with yourself and understand every last bit of your psyche and personality. You need to know what is going on inside your mind and then, use this awareness to motivate yourself and escape the clutches of stress and boredom. If you do not understand yourself, it will be hard to find new goals to inspire and motivate yourself. Meditation remains the best way of discovering this self-awareness.

Meditation:

As a source of energy and focus, nothing quite comes close to touching the effectiveness of meditation. Meditation goes beyond just sitting down, arms folded and closing your eyes while repeating a mantra. As Jiddu Krishnamurti explains the very essence of meditation; "Meditation is to be aware of every thought and every feeling, never to say it is right or wrong, but just to watch it and to move with it". Meditation allows your actions and thoughts to be in perfect synchronization and harmony with what your inner self-desires. This is a quite effective pill for defeating stress. Meditation allows you to catalog the sources of your stress, and file away stress so that it doesn't take you down.

Other effective self-motivation and self-control techniques you can adopt, which include Pilates and Yoga.

CHAPTER 7

BREAK DOWN SELF-BARRIERS, MAKE

YOUR WORLD WIDER

During your marriage, your life had a certain, unique balance brought about by the elements in it: the people. and your actions or habit. Divorce, therefore, takes away one (usually the biggest) factor contributing to this balance. Choosing not to replace a spouse with new activities or other people, therefore, can leave you at the risk of running an unbalanced life that will further strain your levels of resilience. I am not advocating for you to go all out to find a new partner; far from it. But you do need to create better alternatives for your spouse. If you close yourself up and fail to replace him adequately, you run the risk of becoming a lonely recluse with no props to lean upon. You can make your world wider by doing one of the following things:

Do not close your doors to new relationships:

I know you don't want to get burned twice, but that's exactly the reason you need to leave yourself open for new connections to find. If your divorce fills you with so much dread of relationships that you do not take any upon yourself any longer, you would be losing both ways. The one person to soothe your wounds may be out there somewhere, and you can only find him by keeping your doors open. However, do not get so eager in getting back on the horse that you make the same mistakes you made previously. Also, if you have kids, pay adequate attention to their needs and requirements while considering new relationships.

Create new social circles:

Your friends, associates, and peers are an important component of your recovery. Following from the previous point about creating new relationships, you may need to break out of certain circles that remind you of your former husband and join new ones. Of course, you do not just stop talking to his friends and associates, but it may become prudent to take a break from certain friendships you cultivated at his instance. Also, meeting new people can bring its own form of reward.

Make that trip:

What is your dream location for a holiday? Have you always wanted to take a trip down to some Caribbean island or Athens? Do you really love shopping in Paris or a safari in the African jungle? By all means, stop postponing that trip. Just do it. A change of scenery can do you a world of good. Taking time off to enjoy yourself somewhere far away can do wonders for your mood and mind. It absolutely kills stress. By occupying your mind with the beautiful things before you, you can blank out worry.

CHAPTER 8

REFUEL YOUR DREAMS

No matter how much you have prepared before your marriage, it has a way of sneaking in to change our priorities. Where you once had only yourself to think of, you must now consider your partner too. As such, a lot of your pre-marriage dreams may have gone out of the window unnoticed, talk more of being acknowledged. If there is one positive about a divorce, it is the fact that you now have only yourself and possibly your kids to consider. What this means is that you can now explore some of those dreams that you truly cherish. You can pursue them without any fear of being accused of neglect.

Getting back on the trail doing the things you liked but had to abandon, can help you minimize the immediate effects and hassle of your divorce. Your divorce signals a time for you to be yourself once again and enjoy life to the fullest.

Time for new adventures:

The spirit of adventure differs in prominence from individual to individual, but even the least adventurous individual has one or two perfect fantasies she imagines. Try to take on some new adventures that pique your curiosity. Do you love mountain-climbing? Get your backpack and do some climbing. Are you a fan of tennis? Pick up your racket and hit some balls across the local lawn.

Approach every pursuit with positivity:

Not all dreams may be put on hold during your initial marriage. You may have even been encouraged by your spouse. Separation does not mean that those dreams and pursuits have to die. It doesn't matter if they become harder because he is no longer there or reminds you of the times he was. So long as your dreams belong to you, you should remain responsible for them; your divorce can't kill them, only you can.

CHAPTER 9

RELIEVE YOUR STRESS INSTANTLY

BY SWITCHING YOUR ATTENTION

There are many ways and measures to reduce stress and the overall strength of your negative reactions to it, but two, in particular, stand out: a stronger bond with a pet and increasing the attention you pay to your children. Increasing your bonds and relationships with these your children or a pet can help you trounce stress.

Paying attention to your children:

If you have been lucky enough to get children from your marriage, you already have people you can switch attention to as a stress palliative. Catering for your children gives you a daily boost of happiness, pride, and joy that can leave you feeling awesome and grateful for having them. Yes, they can be super annoying and troublesome, all kids are, but wouldn't you rather invest your time in them rather than sulk and ball up your emotions? Shielding your kids from the negative experiences of your divorce is a must though. Do not try to railroad them against their father or you might start a rebellion. Do not try to win them over to your side of the divide by cunning and crafty methods. Instead, take proper care of them and watch them blossom into adulthood in the best of environments.

Adopt a pet:

People adopt pets for various reasons but not everyone knows of the stress-curing effects of having them. Scientific research has shown that owning a pet not only prevents high blood pressure, it also reduces the level of cortisol (the stress hormone), while simultaneously increasing oxytocin (the happiness hormone). People with pets are also likely to feel less lonely and more assured of them. In any case, pets also mean you will get to exercise even more than before. So, that's more exercise, less loneliness and less stress for pet-owners? What are you still waiting for? Go and get your own pet right now!!!

CONCLUSION

A divorce can be a quite messy affair. It can leave you feeling jaded, thoroughly devastated and confused. It heaps a large amount of stress on you in a way that very few things can. And that is exactly why you must learn to manage and deal with this stress to prevent your lifestyle from tumbling downhill and being plunged into chaos. Failure to manage the stress effectively could lead to various distress and health problems (such as depression, addictions, and ulcers) and affect your overall personality. Luckily, with the right mindset and actions, it is easy to survive and grow to leave the claws of your divorce behind you. The most important thing to remember is that you are responsible for yourself; you need to let go of your failed marriage and learn to develop as an individual to become even better. Do not close yourself up. Meet new people, interact, take on new adventures and banish all worry and thoughts of your broken marriage. Always remember, life after divorce is not about him, it is not about your marriage, it is about you and you alone!!!

I want to thank you and congratulate you for buying this book!